GOLF SUCKS

Copyright © 2012, Jack Weltner, MD

All rights reserved.

Cover and interior design by Linda Enrico

Illustrations by Conor Plunkett

GOLF SUCKS *...and then you die!*

Jack Weltner, MD
Illustrated by Conor Plunkett

Dedication

To Laura Plunkett who co-created every stage of this book, from conception through delivery.

To David (of good character) Hark who has accompanied me to so many courses and remained calm despite double bogies, eagles and his hole in one.

And to my wife Linda who has tolerated her days as a golf widow with grace and charity.

Table of Contents

	Introduction
Hole One	Golf is Character
Hole Two	Can You Hold on to Your Dreams?
Hole Three	Focus
Hole Four	Swing from Deep Inside
Hole Five	Oh, What's the Point?
Hole Six	Be a Sponge
Hole Seven	Notice the Beauty
Hole Eight	We Fall Short
Hole Nine	Wrapping Up

Some people think that golfers enjoy their play. Such people are not golfers.

We golfers are rarely happy playing, or even satisfied. The whole concept of "par" gives it all away. Most of us crave a par, dream of one every time we put a tee in the ground, and only rarely achieve that goal. "Par" sounds like average, something we should expect, right? But for the vast, VAST majority of us, it is a rarity. And for the lucky few with minuscule handicaps, they crave birdies, therefore remaining as disappointed as the average Joe like me. Golf is about disappointment, frustration, even humiliation. Not fun.

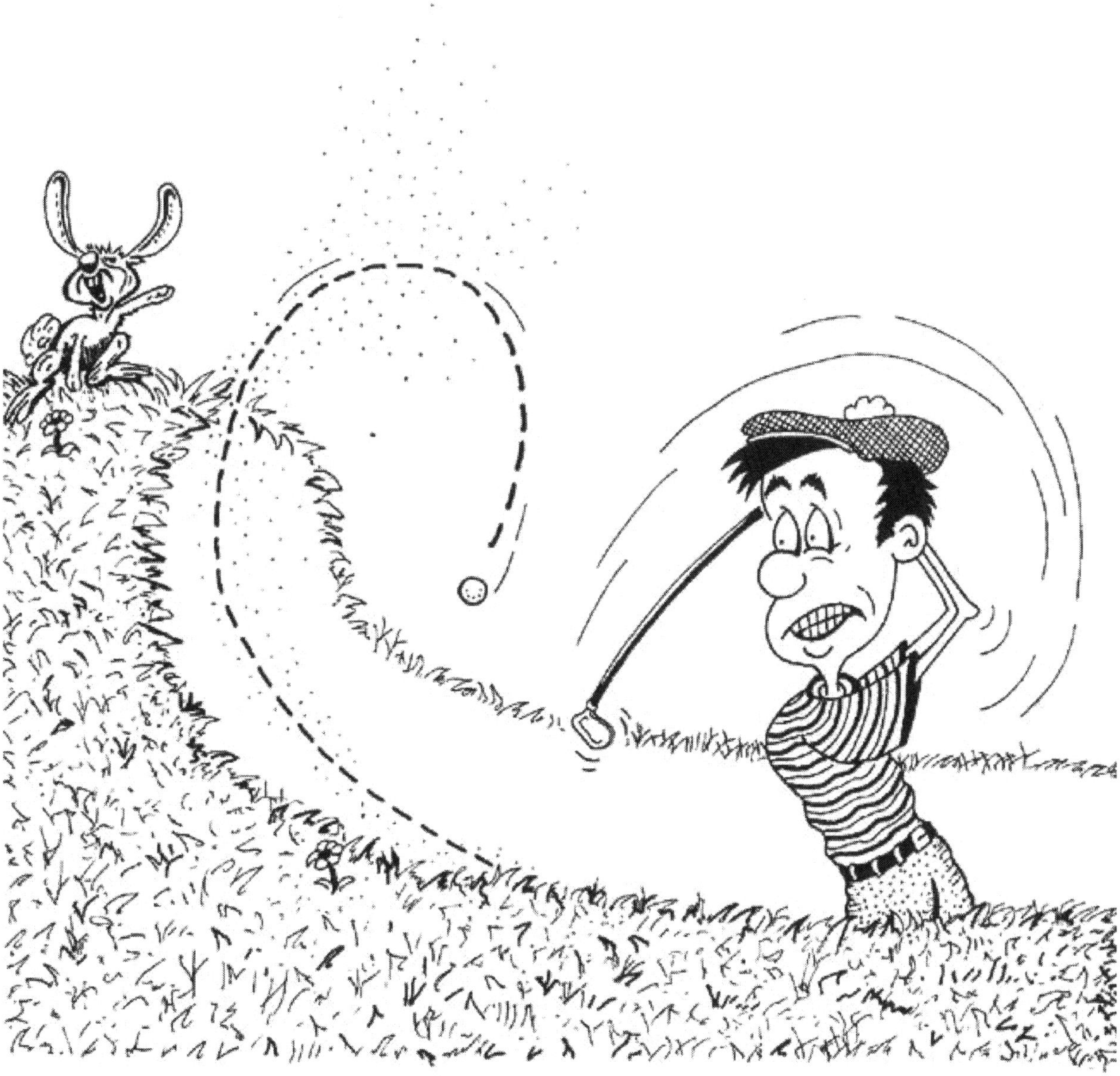

Golf is often misperceived as a social experience, but for the average golfer like me, the only topic is the next shot or the one we just screwed up. Awareness of our colleagues mainly occurs if we are playing a match. Peak conversation is "I'm two holes up on you."

Elation or joy is very rare – the hole in one, the 26 foot putt, the occasional extra-long drive do bring brief moments of happiness. But the bellowed curse, the club slammed into the turf, the pledge to never play "this damned game again" are more common and heartfelt.

Despite this, we golfers keep at it, claim we love the sport, abandon our wives, children and hard-earned money as often as possible. Why?

Having played golf for over 60 years, I consider myself an expert. Not at golf, but at the mystery, the allure of it.

It reminds me of the quest for the Holy Grail. Men spent lifetimes searching empty-handed, but drawn by the elusive hope of some day finding such a treasure. My quest, at 77, is to hit my age. I can hit 80, and do most years. Ten years ago, age 67, I hit a 74. See, there is hope! Just a few lucky putts. Already this year I've had 39's on the front nine twice... and then fallen apart.

Now some cynics point out that it is a silly, boring game. Taking a stick, hitting a ball across a wide field into a little hole is stupid. I see their point. But anything is only exciting if we make it important. Some people are devoted to making money, social status, collecting stamps. The more we are devoted to a pursuit, the more exciting, frustrating and intriguing it becomes.

Unfortunately, I am devoted to golf.

Don't play golf!!

If you're a child and haven't started, avoid it like the plague!

If it's too late

and you've already wasted meaningless hours chasing a small white ball with frustration and disappointment as your constant friend, **this book is for you.**

HOLE ONE

GOLF IS CHARACTER

MITCH DAVID RICH JACK

On to the first hole. I am full of excitement. I am praying for a 77, my age. I am bursting with hope. It's an easy par 5 (456 yards). A few practice swings. I address the ball. Smooth backswing. Whoosh!

Disaster…. The ball pops off the tee into the deep rough. Am I crushed? No! I decide on a mulligan. Much better. Down the middle over 200 yards.

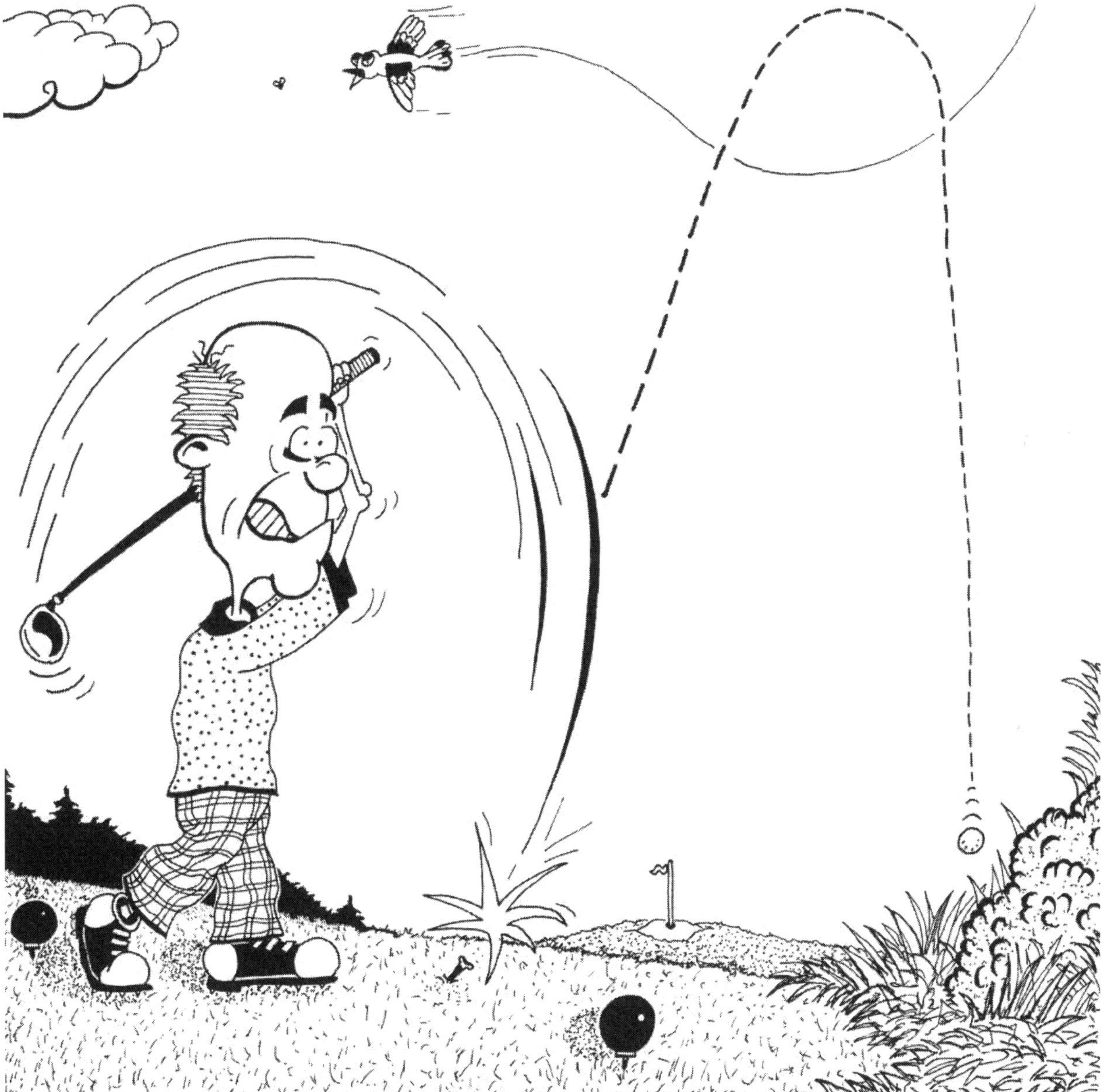

My partner David steps up. He also slices off the fairway into the rough. But David does not take the mulligan I offer. David is of Good Character. He looks a little grim, but he accepts his allotted fate. David is universally known to be honest, kind, trustworthy. He bears adversity without complaining. He is universally loved.

Because of all this, his business and his life are very successful. I like playing with David, even though he notices when I forget a stroke when putting down my score.

Me, I prefer mulligans on the first hole. Why suffer when it is so easy to just start over?

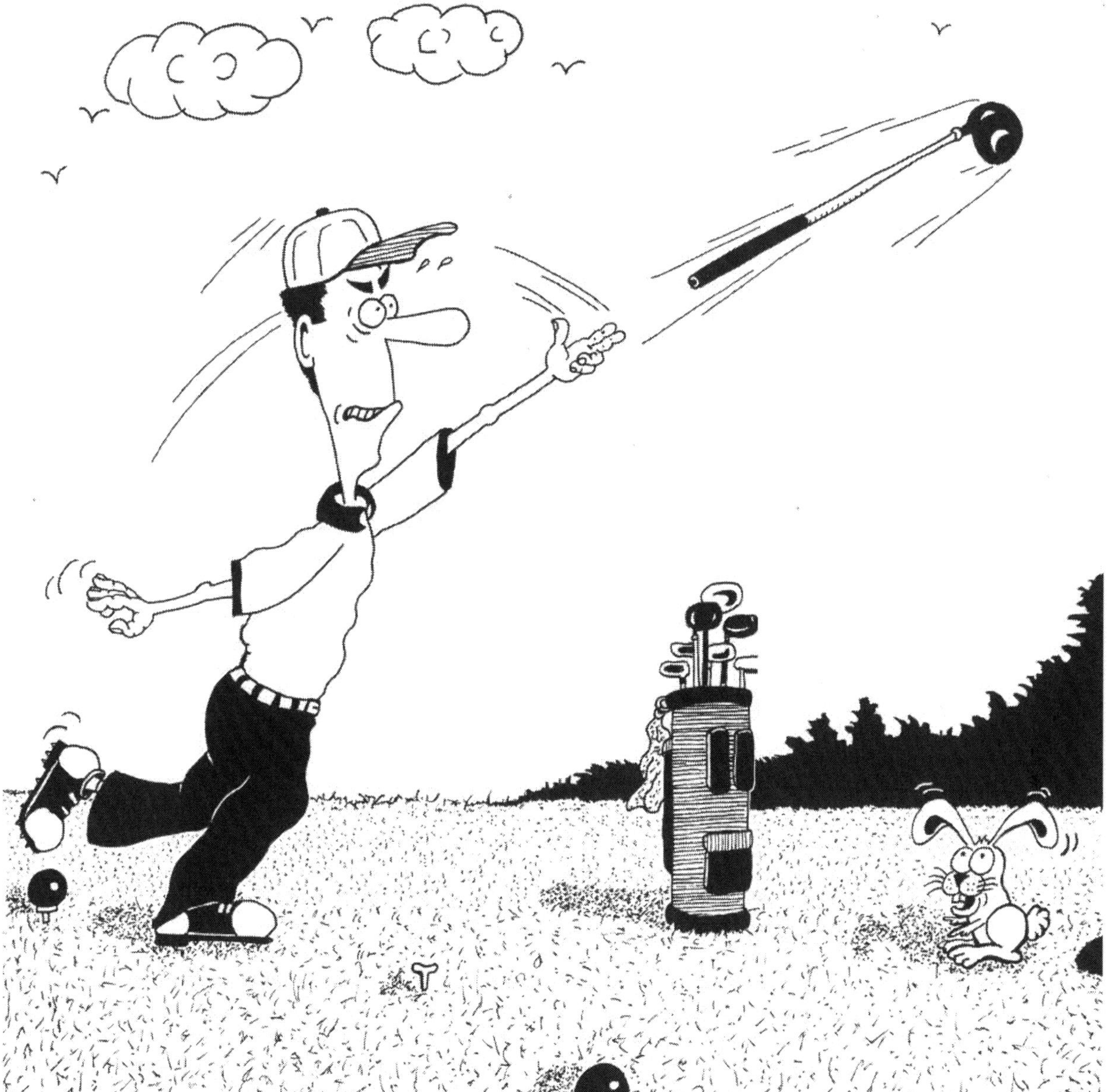

Richard does not suffer quietly. When his drive goes into the trees to the left of the fairway, he throws his club across the tee, looks up accusingly at the heavens, and swears. He will glower his way down the first fairway and fill the air with his "Can you believe that?!"

Mitch, our fourth, tees up. He places his tee and ball about a foot in front of the blue markers. For his second shot, he moves his ball to a better lie in the rough. He will probably declare that his three foot putt on the green is a "gimme".

Now, I am a psychiatrist. I can learn more diagnostically in a round of golf with a person than I could gather in hours in my office. Freud said that our basic self shows up in everything we do. Especially golf. We could guess that David does not complain at home, that he shows up on time, that his behavior is honorable. Richard must be volatile, feels put upon by life, and is outraged at social injustice. As for Mitch, I'll bet he cheats on his income tax.

Me? I am an eternal optimist, always trying to find ways to avoid the miseries. I pretend that life is full of roses without thorns. I am generally out of touch with grim reality. Golf, however, really brings it home. Maybe that is good for my soul.

Sadly, each of us messes up at least one shot, so there are no pars this hole.

Rule 1:
The more misery you can endure, the more holes you will find bearable or positive.

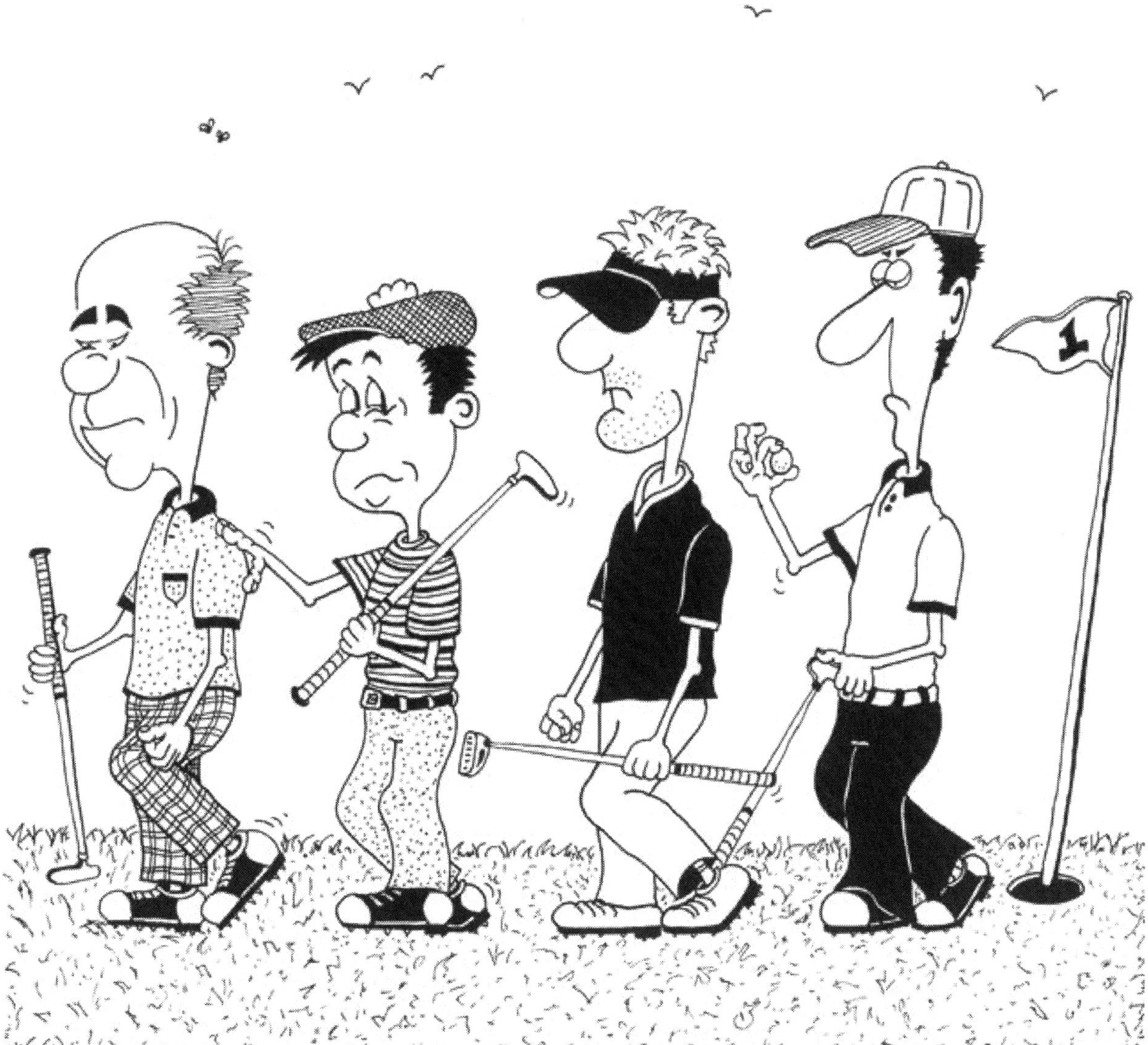
1

HOLE TWO

Can you Hold on to Your Dreams?

We drag off to the second tee. The hole is a medium length par four. There is a tree on the left side of the fairway out about 150 yards. The first hole wasn't much fun and my dream of hitting 77 is slipping away. But I start dreaming of hitting my first birdie, so my mood is improving by the second. David is hunkering down. Rich is still muttering. Mitch is buoyed up as he is keeping score and gave himself a six.

Rule 2:
Golf sucks...
but let's keep hope alive.

Chasing first tee dreams and watching them fade is an everyday issue in golf. Like the rest of life, it was supposed to work out smashingly, but seems to have changed its mind. More holes to come. These next eight holes are a chance to renew hope, despite all odds being against it. The game is definitely more exciting if we can hold on to our optimism in spite of all the evidence.

The second hole is more of the same. I sliced into the forest on the right. Richard pulled his drive. Mitch gave himself another mulligan and hit the fairway. David, steady as always, hit down the middle, and reached the green on his next shot and made an easy par. He walked lighter to the third tee. My optimism was under attack.

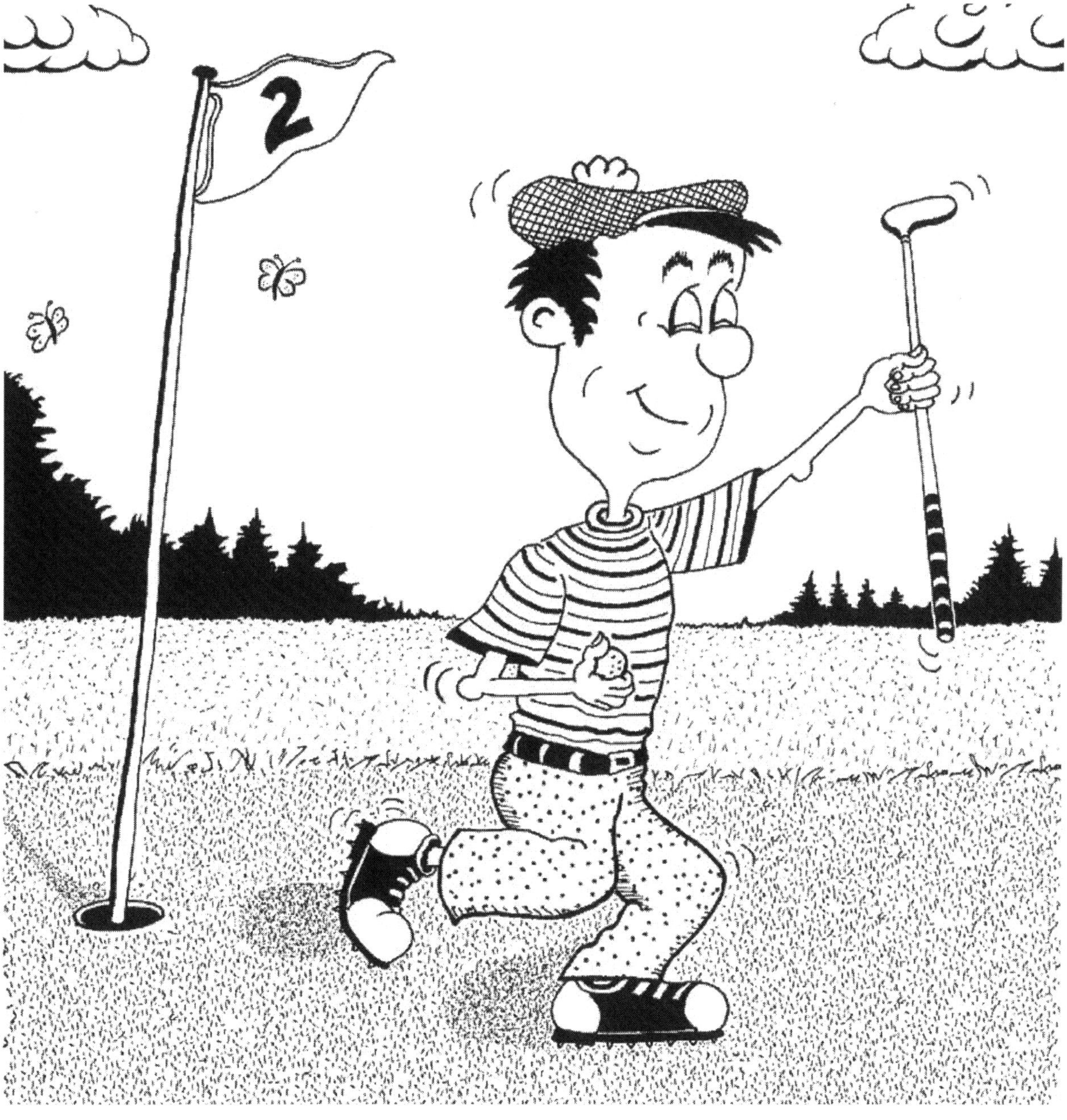
2

HOLE THREE

Focus

But to really enjoy golf, I must stay mindful. Each shot is a new beginning, full of hope and promise. All past blunders are gone. The argument with my wife, the lousy stock market, global warming, the recession, they are also left behind.

I tell myself that what is real is this clean white ball, the green ahead, the feel of the club in my hands. The smooth rhythm of the back swing, the exhilaration of the downswing, the excitement of contact, the flow of the follow-through, this is the whole world in this brief instant. I am determined to be fully alive in the present.

Rule 3:
Every hole is a whole new life, full of promise and hope.

Each hole is an entirely fresh page. This is the magic of golf. Maybe I miss this shot. Maybe I miss most of my shots. But I try to be fully here and stay focused on each shot, waiting for a miracle. I am in a world apart, my separate reality.

This is another par five, and I hit a great drive, a fine three wood, and finally a smooth nine iron close to the pin. I forget both my despair and my elation. I really focus on the putt, and it goes in. A birdie!!! Life is great! Richard misses his putt and curses, but does not throw his putter.

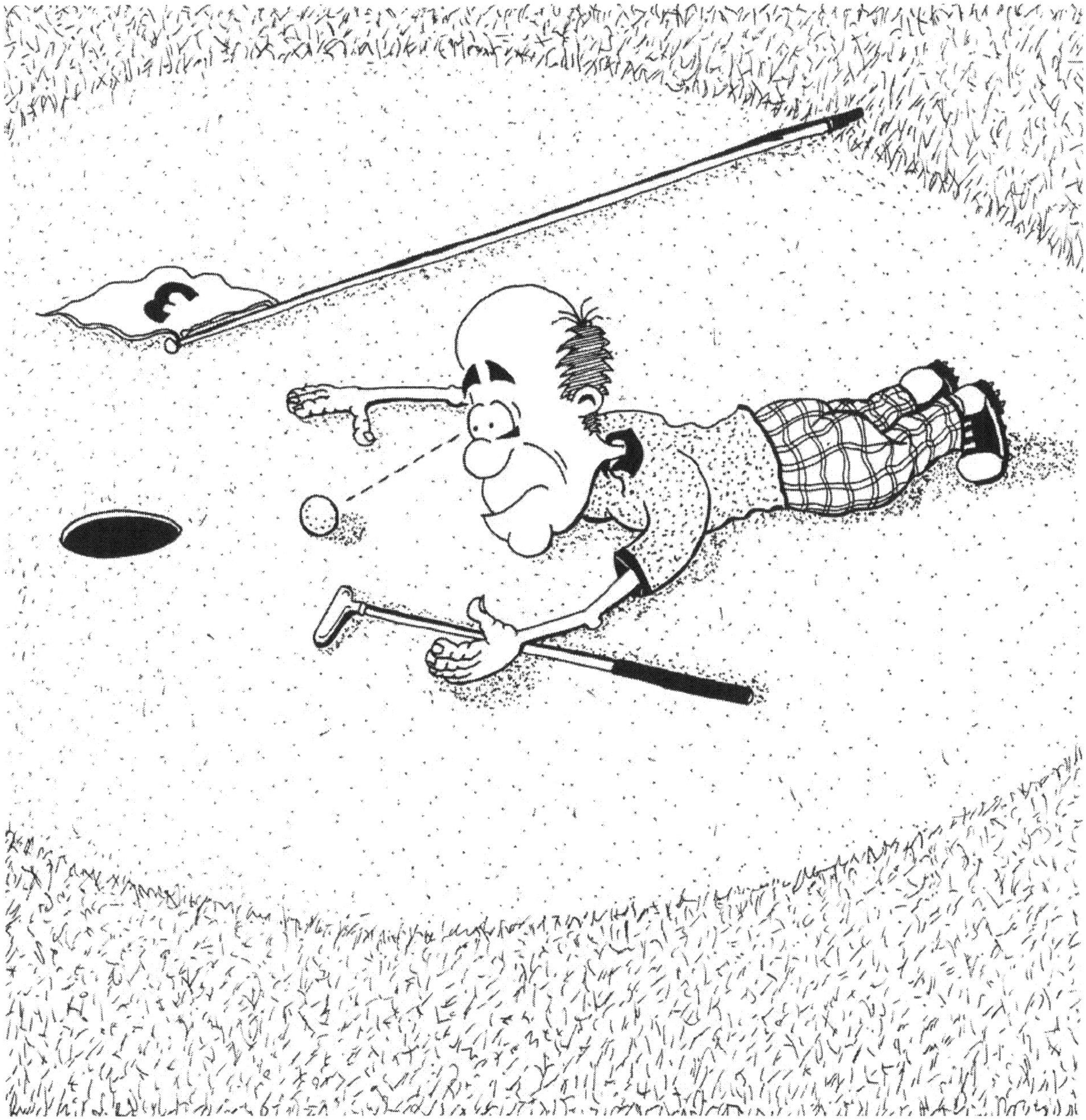

HOLE FOUR

Swing From Deep Inside

Heading to the fourth tee, I am joyous, but my partners are dejected. Reality sucks! I don't know it yet, but I am about to join them. This par four is not too long, but everything rolls to the left, and I bounce left and out of bounds. Two strokes before I even start the hole! This focusing stuff is really hard, especially when my second drive goes nowhere and my next shot goes only half way up the fairway. My third shot, mercifully, lands on the green. Then I see Mitch kick his ball onto the fairway.

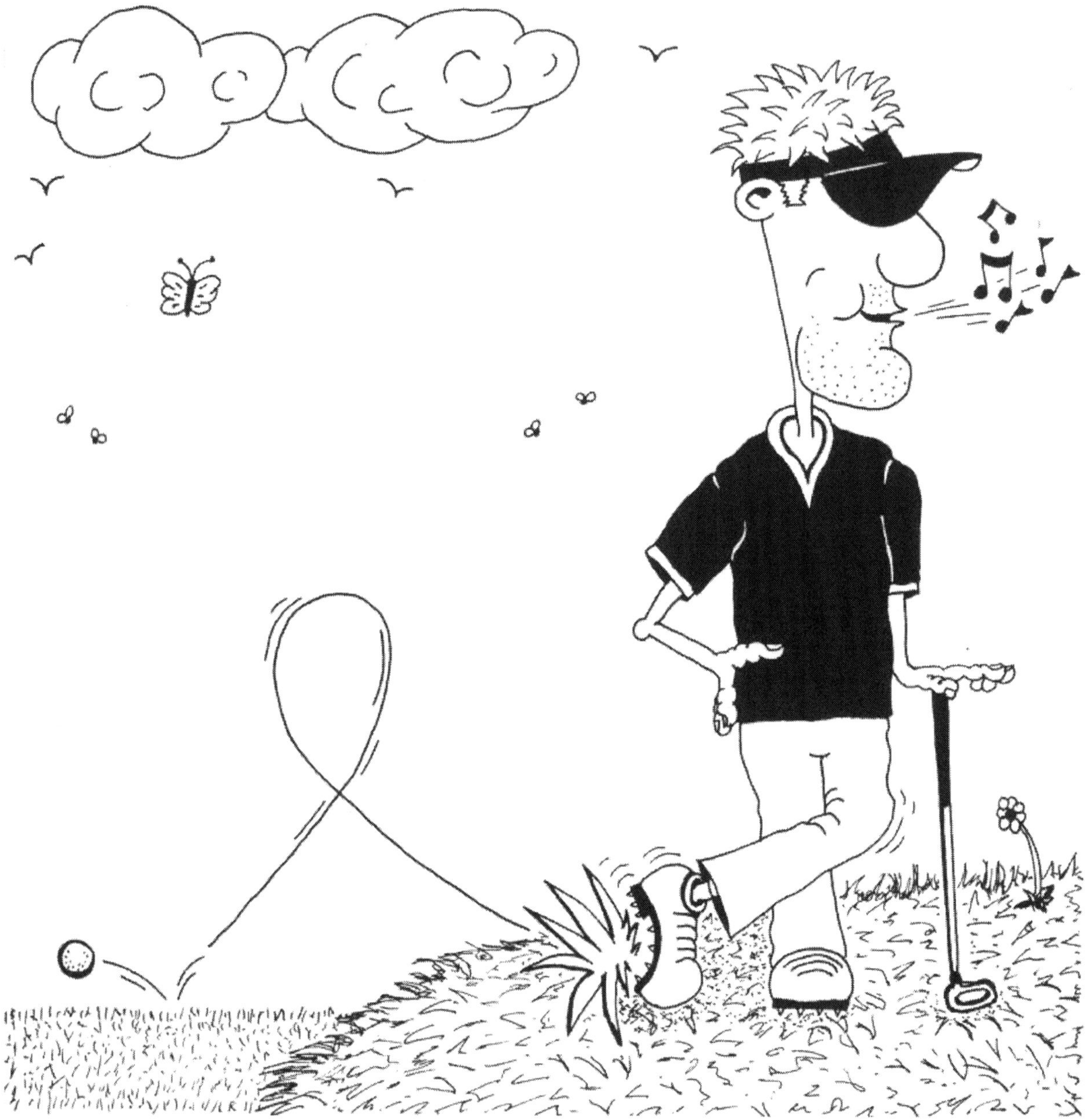

To stay clear, I need to go deeper inside. Often, when I line up a putt, I decide to aim 6 inches left of the cup. Then my hands and putter disobey and the ball heads right and goes in! The putter knows best. That means that there is a part of me that knows better than my brain, and that part takes over. It is clear to me that my mind cannot deal with all the complexity, but that my deep inner golfer can. That inner golfer has been around thousands of greens and maybe for thousands of years, learning many more lessons than my limited intelligence can retain. It is in touch with the flow of the course itself.

So my job is to let that deep knowing run the show. I address the putt and then stay out of it. It goes in! For a six. Mitch gives himself another five.

Rule 4:
When our inner wisdom runs our show, life goes better.

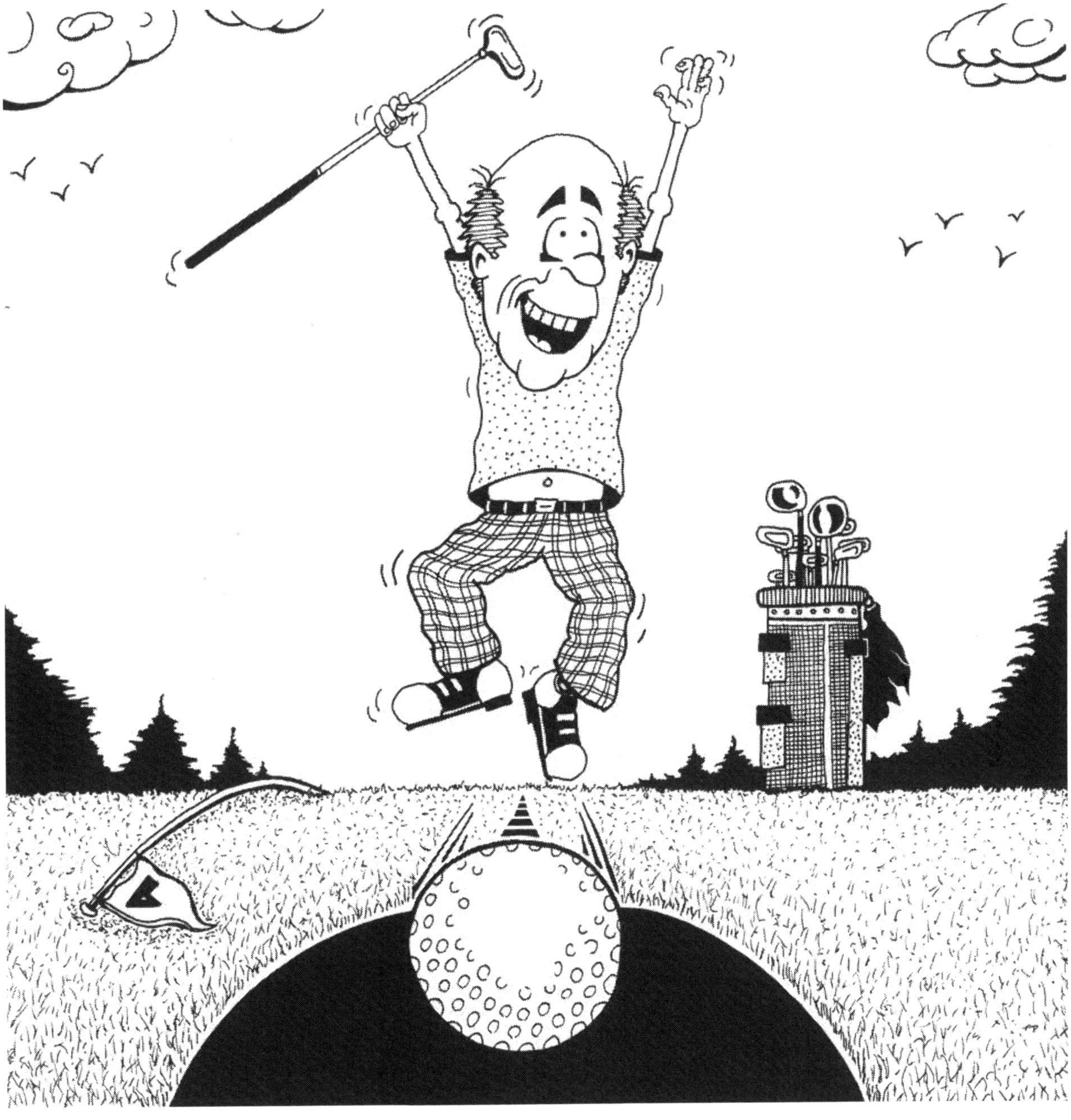

HOLE FIVE

Oh, What's the Point?

We're about half way there now. There's been lots of hacking and a few great shots, but is it worth it? We've invested years in lessons, practicing, buying the newest clubs, the best balls, playing endless rounds, and it comes down to this: chasing a little ball all over this green meadow. I just got another double bogie. What is the point? I think I will give up this damn game.

I need to regroup. This is a birdie hole. Only 295 yards; a decent drive, a nine iron and a one putt! Let's think: am I fully present? Have I let myself appreciate my few good shots? Have I shrugged off the poor shots - "life is difficult" - and moved on emotionally? When I stay enmeshed in bad outcomes and pay attention to my aching back, each round turns into drudgery.

So I address the ball, fresh and present, and Behold. My shot goes long, right down the middle. Hope is reborn! Each of my partners also tees off well. We each hit the green on our second shots. Richard sinks his twenty foot putt for a birdie. He looks to the heavens with a smile. The rest of us all par. Life is worth living after all.

Rule 5:
Every shot, like every dear friend, is a treasure.
Let them go deep inside.

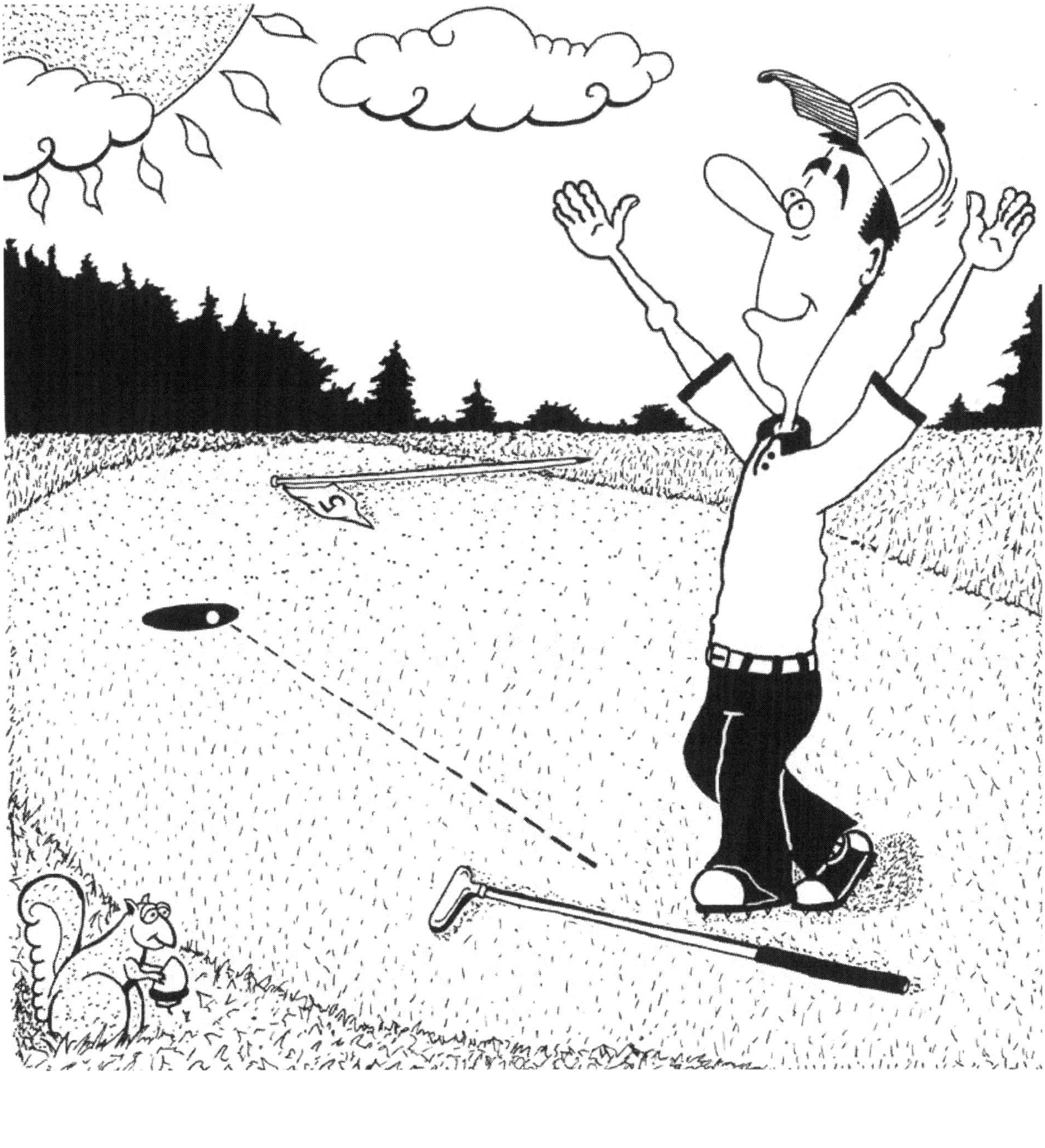
5

HOLE SIX

Be a Sponge

This is a par three and only 170 yards. There is a tree about forty yards in front of the left side of the green. The pin is right behind it. I could get anxious and mess up again. I need to forget that tree. I remember some advice a wise pro gave me:

Rule 6:
Be like a sponge. Come to this present hole empty. Then, carefully and fully, take in the lay of the land; the distance to the green, the wind, the chance you will slice or draw, any past experience of this hole. Take it all in. But finally, when you are full of preparation, dying for release, let it all go. Act. Enjoy the power of the swing.

This is the joy of play; the alternation of methodical planning, thinking everything through and then giving yourself fully to action. Just this, not the result. The result may be sensational or disastrous, but the essence is in the rhythm of filling up and letting go, acting with your whole heart. To hell with outcome. "Thy will be done".

I hit the tree and wind up with a four. David, of good character, aims for the right side of the green and almost sinks his putt. Mitch, who loses his ball and then misses the green, gives himself a five. I notice, but trying for sainthood, say nothing. Richard, the lion-hearted, fuming for all of us, speaks up, "That was a six!" I watch as Mitch adds a thin line making his five into a barely visible six.

SCORECARD
HOLE 6 · PAR 3
BLUE TEE = 170 YDS

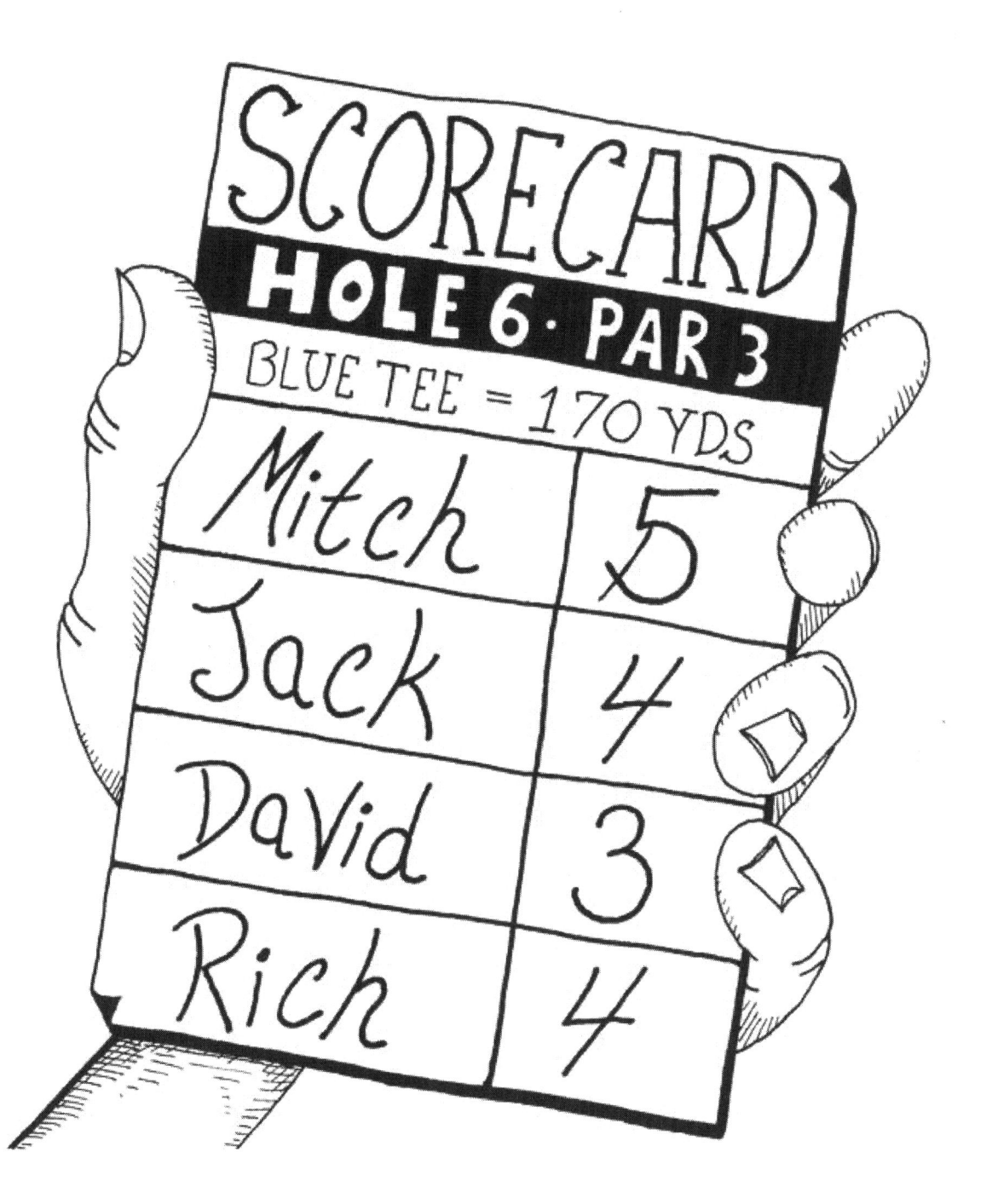

Mitch	5
Jack	4
David	3
Rich	4

HOLE SEVEN

Notice the Beauty

This is a dog-leg to the left. Not too long. Easy to fade into the rough, though.

But I am beginning to notice the beauty that surrounds us. Where else can you see the real slope of the land, its valleys, its rolling hills, these lush green expanses of fairway? In our congested lives, this is as close as we are likely to get to really seeing the earth in all its glory. And the wildlife: this course is home to red-tailed hawks, occasional hedgehogs, chipmunks, squirrels. It has a small herd of deer. Often I see a doe with her small fawn loping just thirty yards away.

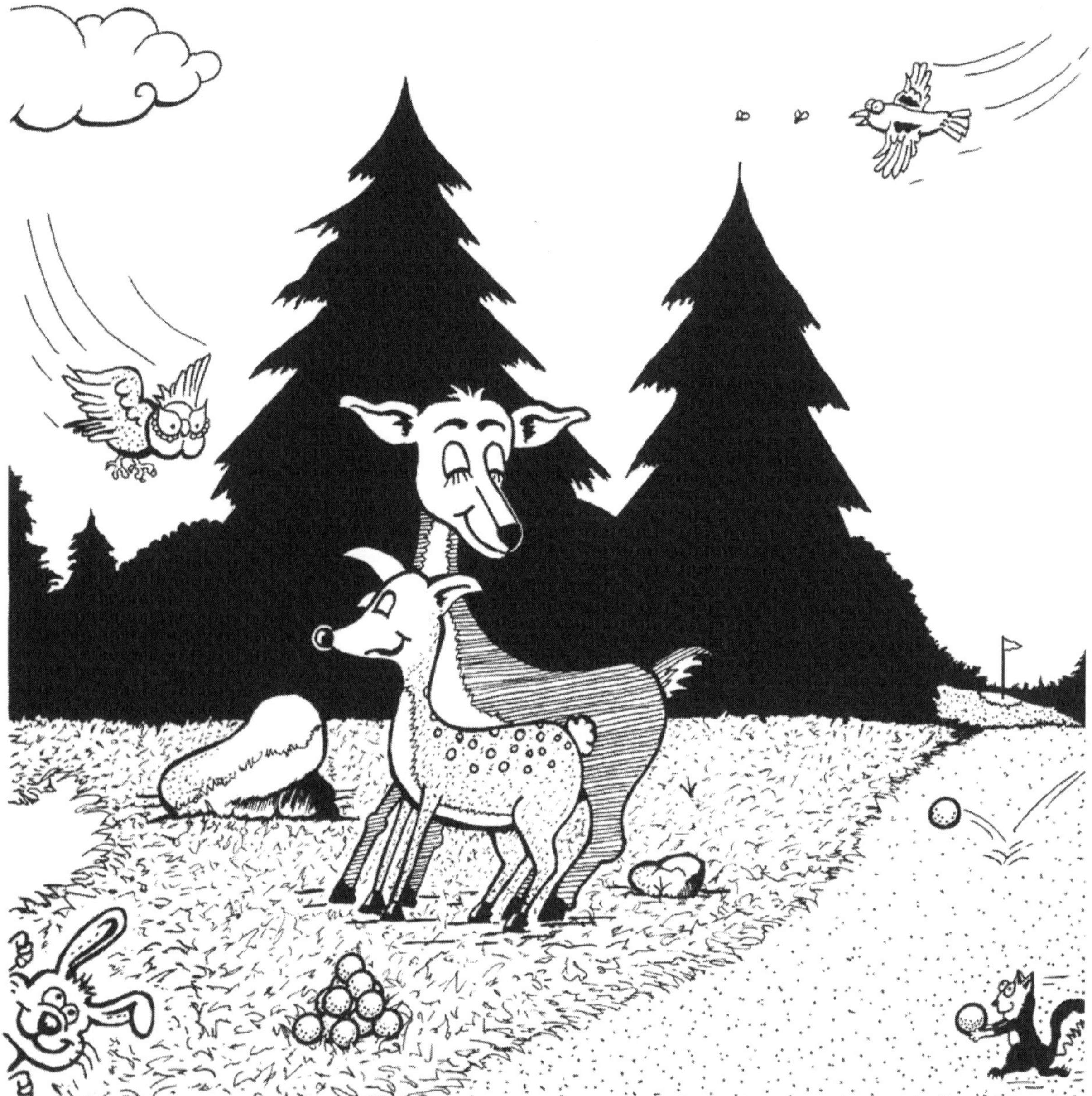

Rule 7:

Be grateful. Noticing how lucky you are to be able to walk this glorious, green meadow creates awareness of being nurtured. Recalling the straight long drives, the sunk putts, is the source of deep well being. Without noticing these things, we can be immersed in all of this goodness but still starve psychologically. But even the worst round provides great gifts to us, if we notice.

Oh yeah?? Despite all my gratitude, I fade and it goes into the rough. Richard, still thanking God for his birdie, puts his drive right down the middle and finishes with the only par.

HOLE EIGHT

We Fall Short

This is one of the prettiest holes on the course: a medium par three, at 190 yards, ending in a green surrounded by tall pines. David and I both roll up to the back of the green, but it slopes down wickedly, so the putting is difficult. Despite all our care and prayers, we both three putt. Richard explodes as he misses his two footer. Mitch gives himself his putt, avoiding a five.

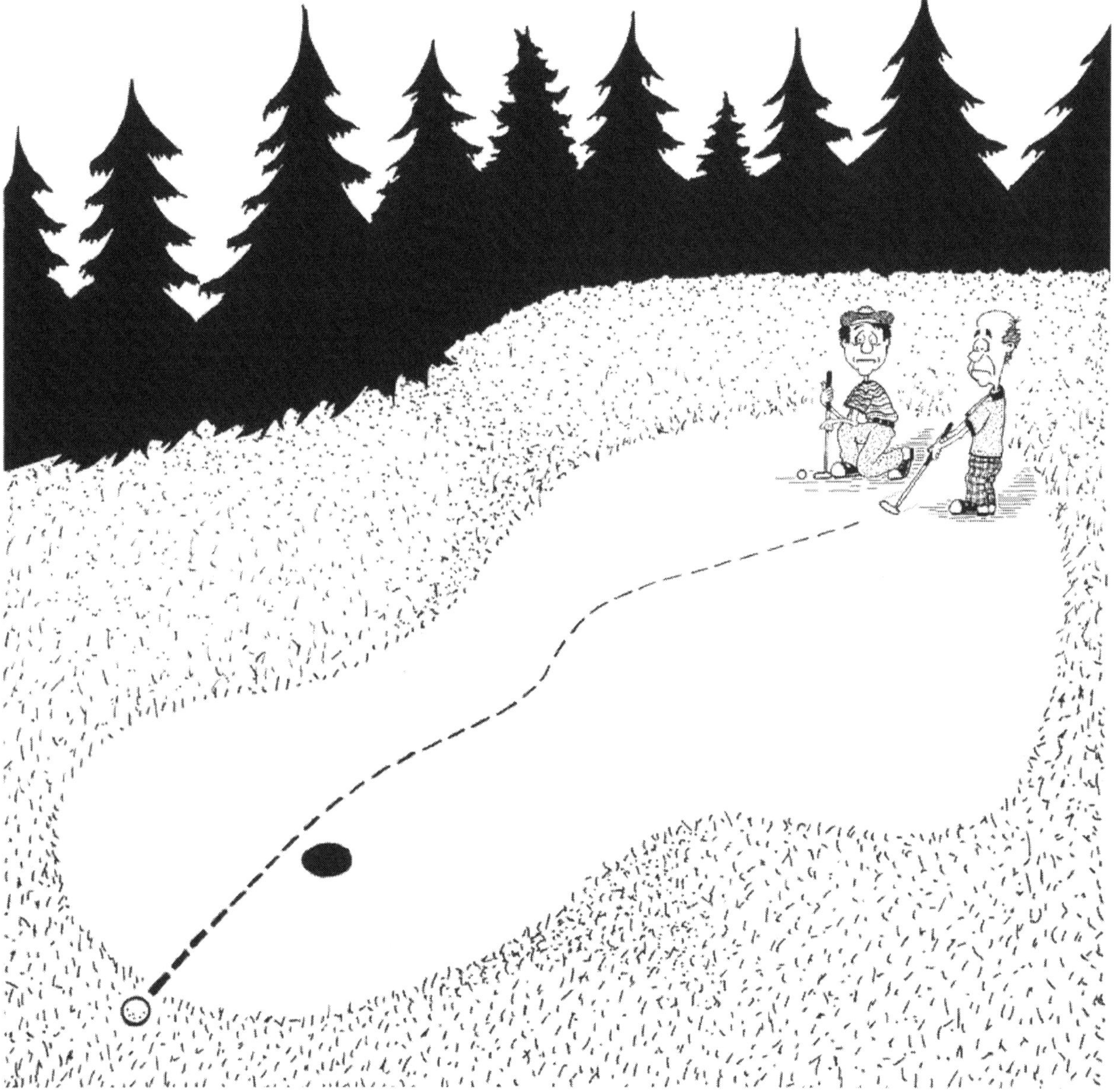

As we walk over to the ninth and final tee, David and I struggle to maintain the elation of our very good drives. It's hard to forget the three putts. We both want to do better, get lots of pars. Two putting isn't so much to ask!

The trouble with golf is that no matter how well I do in this game, I could always do better. It is a real test of self-acceptance. In reality, I'm not that good at putting, and I need to be okay with that. I am probably lovable just as I am. But, as a true golfer, I want to be better. Even if I score in the seventies, I would still be expecting a sixty nine. Learning to love who I really am is a major life goal.

> **Rule 8:**
> **Learning to love who we really are is THE major life goal.**

HOLE NINE

Wrapping Up

The eighth hole was only 190 yards. This final par 3 is 210 yards and uphill. None of us reaches the green. Mitch kicks his ball out of the trees, closer to the green. Richard, closest to the green, chips within a foot of the pin and gets our only par. Somehow, Mitch, though the worst player, cards a 41, low score. David, at 42, withholds comment. Me too.

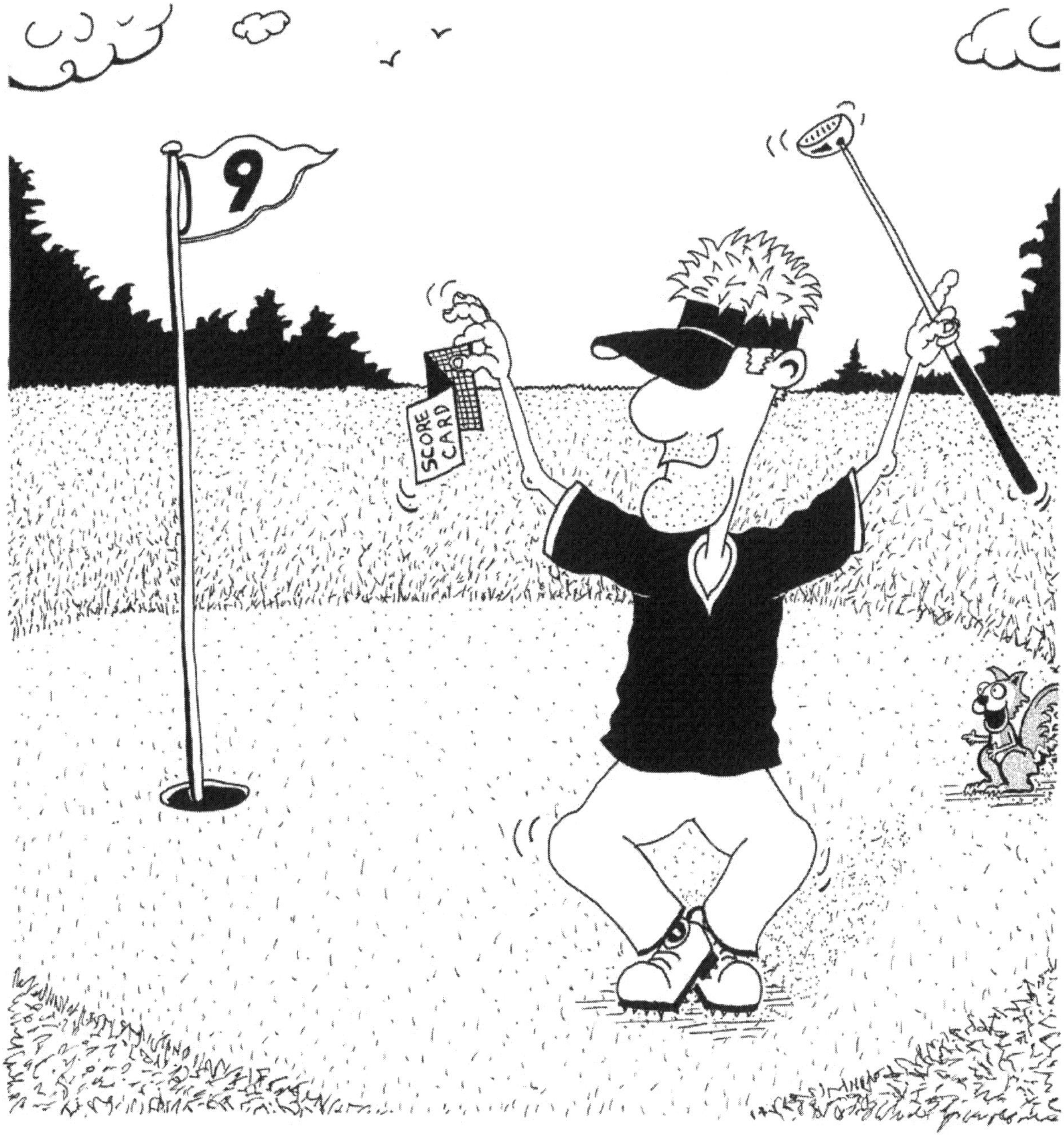
9
SCORE CARD

Well, this round is all over. Now the big choice is how do I feel about it? Was it challenging? Exciting? Did I focus well? I do have a choice. I can remember the four putt and the drive out of bounds, or I can recall my good chip on number seven and the way I hung in after such a bad start on number two. I might be proud, not necessarily of my score, but of how I maintained good spirits despite a mediocre round.

In a life of golf, there will be plenty of missed putts and plenty that go right in. You can try to improve your game, but after many years of trying that one, I have learned to just accept my game and work on getting better at enjoying it.

Enjoying golf, like enjoying life, depends on where you place your attention. In our family, after a few years of hearing our teen-aged daughters' complaints about their day, we all agreed to start each meal by recalling one good thing for which we were grateful. Over time, this practice changed everything.

Rule 9:
These rules apply to golf and to every part of your life.

Jack Weltner, MD is a Harvard trained child psychiatrist who has devoted his career to patient care, as well as teaching individual, child and family therapy at a variety of Boston's venerable institutions. Although he has written numerous professional articles, this is his first venture into writing about his oldest passion, golf. Starting at age 13, Jack has played as often as work and decency allowed. At 77, he has begun a new pursuit – hitting his age. Rarely, he has scored in the seventies. But he has managed to hit an 80 every year for twenty or thirty years. He figures, at 77, he has only a few more years to wait. Off the course, he and wife Linda created two lovely daughters, both therapists and four grandchildren.

Let us know what you think. We'd love to hear from you!

Jack Weltner: jackweltner@yahoo.com, 781-631-8581
For more inspiration from Jack, go to: safe-harbor.cc
To order copies of this book: safe-harbor.cc/golfsucks.htm

Conor Plunkett: conplunkett@gmail.com, 508-429-5035

Linda Enrico: linda@enricodesign.com, 781-631-2520

Acknowledgements

I am deeply grateful to Linda Enrico who has skillfully taken my manuscript and created this attractive book. And to Conor Plunkett, cartoonist, who brought forth our four golfers from the depths of his imagination. Author Andy Dunlop found all of my numerous grammatical and spelling errors and abolished them. He also laughed a lot when he read this. My daughter Laura Plunkett encouraged me to write this, and has supported, encouraged and cheered me throughout. My neighbor, Henry Hammond, an author, read an early version and made helpful suggestions that reshaped this book. It did take a village.

18
JACK
WELTNER
1934–2034
HE REFUSED
TO DIE
UNTIL HE
HIT HIS AGE

Made in the USA
Charleston, SC
09 September 2012